VERMONT

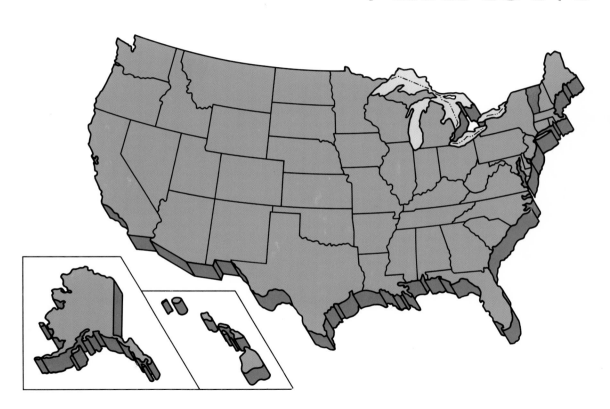

VERMONT

Kathy Pelta

Lerner Publications Company

Cover photograph courtesy of Jamie Cope / Vermont Department of Travel & Tourism.

The glossary on page 69 gives definitions of words shown in **bold type** in the text.

LIBRARY OF CONGRESS
CATALOGING-IN-PUBLICATION DATA
Pelta, Kathy.
    Vermont / Kathy Pelta.
      p. cm. — (Hello USA)
    Includes index.
    ISBN 0-8225-2729-4 (lib. bdg.)
    1. Vermont—Juvenile literature. [1. Vermont.]
I. Title. II. Series.
F49.3.P45 1995
974.3—dc20   93-33389
                          CIP
                          AC

CONTENTS

Factory workers in Vermont stack slabs of marble.

Did You Know . . . ?

❑ In 1977 fourth graders from Barnard, Vermont, chose the honeybee as the state insect.

❑ Students learning to be chefs in Montpelier, Vermont, baked the cake for President Bill Clinton's 1993 inauguration party in January. Made in the shape of the United States, the cake was nine feet (three meters) long!

❑ Vermont's marble has been used in many famous buildings, such as the Supreme Court in Washington, D.C. Some of Vermont's marble is ground up for use in paints, plastics, and even chewing gum!

☐ Millions of years ago, reptiles known as plesiosaurs swam in Vermont's Lake Champlain. Some people say that Champ, the lake's fabled long-necked monster, may be a descendant of these reptiles.

☐ The first globe in the United States was made in 1799 by Vermonter James Wilson. Other inventions from Vermont include the rubber eraser, the steel carpenter's square, and the platform scale.

A Trip Around the State

The name Vermont comes from the French words *vert,* for "green," and *mont,* for "mountain." Vermont's tree-covered ranges run north to south down the center of the small state, giving it the nickname the Green Mountain State.

At one time, Vermont's mountains were twice as high as they are now. About 80,000 years ago, huge masses of ice called **glaciers** inched slowly across much of North America. The weight and force of the glaciers sculpted Vermont's peaks and carved its valleys. When the ice melted, it filled low areas, creating lakes and rivers.

Autumn leaves *(above)* **brighten the Green Mountains** *(facing page).*

9

Lake Champlain is Vermont's largest lake.

Vermont is part of New England, a region in the northeastern United States that once belonged to Britain. Vermont's northern neighbor is the Canadian province of Quebec. Massachusetts is to the south of Vermont. The long Connecticut River forms the boundary between Vermont and its eastern neighbor, New Hampshire. To the west is New York, with Lake Champlain marking part of the border.

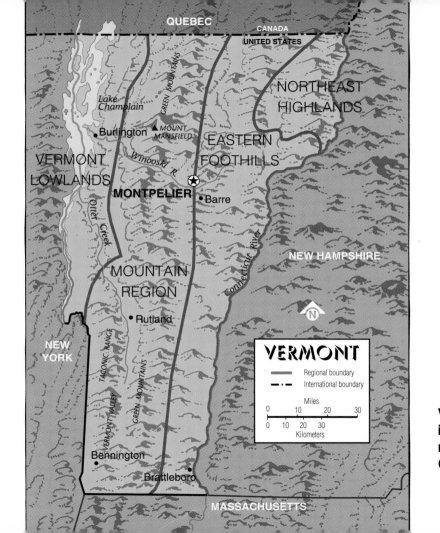

QUEBEC

CANADA

UNITED STATES

NORTHEAST HIGHLANDS

Lake Champlain

GREEN MOUNTAINS

• Burlington

▲ MOUNT MANSFIELD

EASTERN FOOTHILLS

Winooski R.

VERMONT LOWLANDS

★

MONTPELIER

• Barre

Otter Creek

Connecticut River

NEW HAMPSHIRE

MOUNTAIN REGION

• Rutland

N

NEW YORK

TACONIC RANGE

GREEN MOUNTAINS

VERMONT VALLEY

VERMONT

⎯⎯ Regional boundary

–·–· International boundary

Miles

0   10   20   30

0   10   20   30

Kilometers

• Bennington

• Brattleboro

MASSACHUSETTS

Vermont is the only state in New England that does not border the Atlantic Ocean.

11

A black-bear cub clings to a tree.

Vermont has four land regions—the Northeast Highlands, the Eastern Foothills, the Mountain Region, and the Vermont Lowlands. Granite mountains and swiftly flowing streams cover the Northeast Highlands. In the thick forests roam moose, white-tailed deer, and black bears. Sand and loose rock left by glaciers make the soil poor for farming. Logging is the region's main industry.

South and west of the Northeast Highlands are the rolling hills, valleys, and farms of the Eastern Foothills. In the valleys, farmers grow apple trees and raise dairy cattle. To the west, the foothills gradually rise to meet the ranges of the Mountain Region.

Hikers climb Camels Hump in the Green Mountains.

Two major mountain chains rise in the Mountain Region. The Green Mountains, called the backbone of Vermont, stretch the entire length of the region. Rabbits and foxes dart through the forests, which are also home to woodchucks, mink, and porcupines. Mount Mansfield, the highest point in the state, rises 4,393 feet (1,339 m) in the Green Mountains.

The Taconic Range, also in the Mountain Region, extends along the state's western border. The long, narrow Vermont Valley separates the Taconics from the Green Mountains. Miners have dug **quarries,** or deep pits, to reach the large stores of limestone and marble that lie under the valley.

13

At its northern end, the Vermont Valley widens into the Vermont Lowlands, often called the Champlain Valley. Much of this region is sandwiched between Lake Champlain to the west and the Green Mountains to the east. Crops thrive in the fertile soil of the Vermont Lowlands. Burlington, the state's largest city, is located in this region.

Otter Creek, Vermont's longest river, flows north across the lowlands and empties into Lake Champlain. Several large rivers, including the Winooski, flow west into Lake Champlain from the Green Mountains. Other waterways run eastward from the Green Mountains and join the Connecticut River.

Vermont's summers are usually warm, with temperatures between 70° and 80° F (21° and 27° C). Summer thunderstorms can hit fast, pelting areas with rain and hail. The state's yearly

Vermonters buy fresh produce at a farmers' market in Burlington.

14

precipitation, or rain and melted snow, averages 39 inches (99 centimeters). Around the middle of October, the first frost hardens the ground, and Vermont's oak and maple leaves turn brilliant shades of red and gold.

Winters are long and harsh in Vermont, with an average temperature of 22° F (–6° C). Heavy snow and ice blanket the state for months. The Vermont Lowlands receive about 60 inches (152 cm) of snow each year. Some places in the mountains get twice as much, attracting thousands of skiers.

Skiers enjoy the snowy slopes in Vermont.

A group of Vermonters try to free a vehicle stuck in the mud during the mud season.

The warm days of early spring bring out blossoms on fruit trees, and wildflowers brighten the land. Heavy rainstorms in spring combine with melting snow to produce Vermont's "fifth season"—one of mud! Although the mud season doesn't last long, mucky dirt roads often bring traffic to a standstill. Schools in the countryside sometimes close until the roads dry out.

In late spring, the landscape turns from brown to many shades of green, with grassy meadows, forests of evergreens, and newly leafed birch, maple, and beech trees. Residents call this time the greening of Vermont.

Wildflowers bloom throughout Vermont in spring.

Vermont's Story

The Abenaki harvested corn in the fall and stored some of the crop in cellars for a winter food supply.

The first people to explore what is now Vermont were hunters who stalked their prey in mountains and forests thousands of years ago. By the year A.D. 1300, descendants of the early hunters had settled in valleys, where they grew crops. This Native American nation, called the Abenaki, lived in villages east of what is now Lake Champlain. These Indians named the lake Petoubouque.

The villagers arranged their daily tasks to fit the seasons. Spring was the time to plant beans, corn, and squash. Women and children gathered nuts and berries for food and medicine.

Abenaki Indians hunted near the shores of Petoubouque Lake.

Villagers planted corn (above) **and boiled tree sap for syrup** (below).

During warm weather, Abenaki families sometimes left their villages for weeks at a time to fish and hunt. They fished for salmon and trapped porcupines and squirrels. With bows and arrows, the hunters shot larger animals, such as moose and deer. Some Abenaki left home during the summer to exchange shells and arrowheads with members of nearby nations.

During the cold winters, villagers stayed close to home and survived on stored foods, such as corn and dried meat. The women sewed animal hides to make clothing and moccasins, while the men repaired tools and weapons.

The Abenaki got along with nearly all of their neighbors. But the Iroquois, who lived on the west side of Petoubouque Lake, were enemies of the Abenaki. For many years, these nations fought each other over territory.

Lake Champlain is named for Samuel de Champlain.

In 1609 a French fur trader and explorer named Samuel de Champlain arrived in what is now Vermont. He had traveled by canoe from a settlement in Quebec, New France (now Canada). With him were two other Frenchmen and their Indian guides.

Near Petoubouque Lake, Champlain's group joined a raid against a band of Iroquois. The bows and arrows of the Iroquois were no match for Champlain's musket balls. The Frenchman shot two Iroquois leaders, causing the rest of the group to retreat. Later, the Abenaki persuaded Champlain to attack the Iroquois again. From then on, the Iroquois treated the French as their enemies, too.

When other French settlers reached the Champlain Valley, they put up forts to guard against Iroquois attacks. The first was Fort Sainte Anne, built in 1666 on an island in Lake Champlain.

21

Hunters trapped beavers for their soft, warm fur. The hides were sewn into fashionable hats, which sold in Europe for high prices.

Some of the French settlers were traders who received furs from the Abenaki in exchange for wool blankets, metal pots, and guns. Along with the traders came **missionaries.** They taught the Abenaki about the Catholic religion and tried to make the Indians give up their traditional beliefs. Settlers disrupted the Abenaki way of life.

Without meaning to, the newcomers brought deadly germs. Unlike the Europeans, the Abenaki had never been exposed to smallpox, measles, cholera, and some other diseases. Nothing the Abenaki healers did could make their people well, and many of the Indians died.

Like the French, the British also had built settlements along the eastern seacoast of North America. Called **colonies,** these settlements included Massachusetts, New Hampshire, and New York, all of which surrounded what is now Vermont. But the British wanted more land. In the

Indians in Vermont sided with the French during the French and Indian War.

early 1700s, they tried to take areas that the French had claimed—but the French fought back.

The clashes between the British and French led to the French and Indian War (1754–1763). The British, with help from the Iroquois, raided French forts and destroyed Abenaki villages in the Champlain Valley. The French and the Abenaki attacked the British settlers in Massachusetts and New York.

Although the war was costly for the British, they defeated the French and the Abenaki. The British then took over most of New France, and settlers from the British colonies began to move into Abenaki territory in the Champlain Valley. Because the settlers invaded the Abenaki's hunting lands, the Indians could no longer provide for themselves as they once had. Most of them left the area.

At this time, both the New York and the New Hampshire colonies claimed the Abenaki homelands. New York's governor gave sections of the land to his friends. Conflicts arose when New Hampshire's governor granted some of the same land to his friends. This disputed territory became known as the New Hampshire Grants, or simply, the Grants.

As more New Hampshire settlers moved into the Grants, New York complained to the British king. In 1764 the king declared that the land belonged to New York. The "Yorkers" then rushed to the Grants to demand rent from the New Hampshire settlers. Those who refused to pay were forced from their homes by Yorker sheriffs.

Some New Hampshirites staged a rebellion and asked a soldier named Ethan Allen for help. Allen and his friends formed a troop called the Green Mountain Boys. Their job was to protect the Grants from the Yorkers.

Heroes or Outlaws?

Ethan Allen, leader of the Green Mountain Boys, was known for being bold and daring. Legends tell of Allen biting iron nails in two and knocking down an ox with one blow of his fist. But these stories were probably made up by the Green Mountain Boys. One thing is known for sure—Allen and his soldiers were brave enough to take on the Yorkers, who had more soldiers as well as the support of the British king.

Some people thought of Ethan Allen and the Green Mountain Boys as heroes, since the troop usually fought with their fists instead of with guns. But others saw them as bullies who refused to obey the law. The Green Mountain Boys roamed the Grants, stomping on the Yorkers' cornfields and burning their houses. The troop bullied Yorker officials by whipping them with sticks. Once, they even put a Yorker in an armchair, lifted him up to a tavern sign, and left him there to dangle for two hours.

As punishment, Yorker officials threatened to hang any troop member who could be captured. But that didn't stop the Green Mountain Boys. The troop continued to protect their territory like fierce mountain lions. They even put a stuffed catamount (mountain lion) above the sign of their meeting place as a warning to all Yorkers. The snarling cat faced west, toward the colony of New York.

Meanwhile, Britain demanded that the settlers pay high taxes. Britain also made new, stricter laws for all the colonies. As a result, many colonists refused to be loyal to the king any longer. By 1775 these events had led to the American Revolution—a war in which the colonies fought to gain their independence from Britain.

Soon after the war began, the Green Mountain Boys raided Britain's Fort Ticonderoga on the western shore of Lake Champlain. Taking the British guards by surprise, the soldiers were able to capture the fort without firing a shot.

Ethan Allen led the capture of Fort Ticonderoga in 1775.

The Battle of Bennington

Two years into the American Revolution, the British army badly needed supplies, such as horses, wagons, weapons, and food. The army intended to restock in the town of Bennington, located in the Grants. Thinking that most of the Grants' residents were loyal to the British king, the soldiers planned to arrive in town and take the items they needed without trouble.

But when the colonists heard that the British soldiers were coming, they armed themselves for battle. Farmers and townspeople gathered alongside the Green Mountain Boys to keep horses and other supplies out of enemy hands. On the outskirts of Bennington, near the New York border, a troop of nearly 2,000 colonists awaited the British army's approach.

On August 16, 1777, the colonists fought against 1,000 British soldiers in the Battle of Bennington. With their victory, the colonists were able to prevent the British army from entering and taking control of what is now Vermont.

Although the Battle of Bennington was actually fought on New York soil, Vermonters take credit for its success. One of the world's largest battle monuments honors the Vermonters who defeated the British that summer day. Located in Bennington, Vermont, the Bennington Battle Monument stands 306 feet (93 m) tall.

While the war raged, people in the Grants were planning for their future. In 1777 they set up their own independent government, adopted the name Vermont, and wrote a **constitution** (set of laws).

Vermont's constitution outlawed slavery and gave all white men the right to vote—even men who were poor or did not own land.

The colonies defeated the British and in 1783 united to form a new

Vermont's flag shows the state's coat of arms on a deep blue background. The tree, cow, and bundles of grain are symbols of Vermont's agriculture.

28

country—the United States of America. Vermonters asked to be admitted to the Union, but Yorkers argued that they owned Vermont. To settle the dispute, Vermont paid New York $30,000 and in 1791 joined the Union as the 14th state.

During its first 10 years as part of the Union, Vermont was the fastest growing state in the nation. New settlers could purchase land at a fair price, and the population grew quickly. For the few remaining Abenaki, however, life was a struggle. Vermonters took over even more of the Abenaki's hunting land. Some of the Indians survived by selling goods to the settlers.

Like the Abenaki before them, Vermont's settlers lived by the seasons. They planted corn, beans, and squash in the spring and harvested in the fall. In the winter, they chopped firewood, made and repaired tools, and cut ice from frozen lakes. With the first spring thaw, they tapped maple trees for sweet sap, which they used to make syrup and candy.

Settlers burned logs for heat and for cooking meals.

To earn extra money, many Vermont farmers chopped down trees and burned them to make potash, a powdery ash used in soap and in fertilizer for crops. In those days, 2,000 pounds (907 kilograms) of wood was needed to make just 7 pounds (3 kg) of potash. By the early 1800s, Vermont's hills were nearly treeless.

On the bare hills, farmers planted apple orchards or raised wheat. But when other states began growing wheat, the competition hurt Vermont's farmers. Some of them left the state after a few dry summers parched their crops.

Hard times continued for Vermont when the United States and Britain went to battle in the War of 1812. At that time, the British navy controlled many shipping routes and would not let the United States deliver goods to France—Britain's enemy. But the United States depended on money earned from overseas trading and fought for the right to trade.

Many Vermonters did not support the war because it halted their trade with British-controlled Canada. Some residents turned to smuggling to get their goods across the Canadian border.

In rushing water, rivermen guided logs to sawmills.

Vermont's trade centered around Lake Champlain. Workers floated logs down rivers to sawmills at the lake's edge. Farmers used the lake to transport their crops and cattle north to Canada. Canada, in turn, shipped goods Vermonters needed, including salt. By 1823 canals had been built, opening new water routes for shippers to haul goods from Lake Champlain south to New York City.

Tools of the Trade

By the 1830s, Vermont's factories were buzzing. Workers used hand tools to pound and shape iron and other metals into everything from rifles to sewing machines to carriages. Factories began to look for ways to make their products more quickly. Before long, Vermonters had invented machine tools, which could drill, grind, cut, and press metal faster and more accurately than people could.

The small town of Windsor, Vermont, became a leader in the U.S. machine tool industry. By 1865 the Windsor Manufacturing Company was producing planers, lathes, punching presses, drills, and other machine tools. The firm later moved to Springfield, Vermont, where workers continued to invent and produce new tools.

Throughout most of the 1800s, Vermont's factory workers built machine tools that were considered the best in the world. As a result, Vermont's factories regularly supplied machine tools to large, out-of-state manufacturers. In this way, Vermont contributed to the growth of factories and businesses all across the nation.

Meanwhile, sheep farmers in the Champlain Valley grew rich by supplying the state's textile (cloth) mills with wool. But when farmers in the western United States and Australia also began producing wool, competition increased and prices dropped. Many sheep farmers in Vermont turned to raising dairy cows. Soon the milk was being made into butter and cheese at dairies across the state.

Some of Vermont's dairy farmers made their own butter.

34

Irish workers built Vermont's railroads.

During the late 1800s, **immigrants** from Ireland laid railroad tracks across Vermont. Trains began carrying the state's butter and cheese to Boston, New York, and other cities in nearby states. The trains also hauled slabs of granite, slate, and marble from Vermont to ports in other states for shipment overseas.

Because trains could carry Vermont's stone to many markets, the state's mining business grew. Companies hired marblecarvers from Italy, slateworkers from Wales, and stonecutters from Spain and Scotland. At the same time, immigrants from Hungary, Poland, Russia, and Canada arrived to work in Vermont's growing factories.

Trains also brought summer vacationers to Vermont. Hotels in the Green Mountains attracted city dwellers with advertisements praising the fresh mountain air and pure springwater. Tourism thrived in the early 1900s, but fewer people were moving to Vermont. For the first time, the state's population dropped.

At this time, about half of all working Vermonters had jobs in factories, mills, or quarries. Others worked in agriculture. Although dairy farms did well, some of Vermont's crop farmers did not make enough money and left to try farming in other states.

Vermonters faced other problems, too. In 1927 floods along the Winooski and Connecticut rivers killed 85 people and destroyed homes, farms, bridges, and roads. Two years later, the state was hit by the Great Depression, a nationwide economic slump that lasted for about 10 years.

During the depression, factories closed in Vermont and across the country. Millions of people lost their jobs. The U.S. government hired some jobless Vermonters to

Four people drowned on this street in Barre, Vermont, when the Winooski River flooded in 1927.

work on flood-control projects, to pave roads, and to plant trees in the state.

The government workers also cut ski trails, and Vermont became a popular area for skiing, sledding, and ice-skating. In 1934 the state's first ski tow began operating on a farm in Woodstock, Vermont. Soon after, the first chairlift carried skiers up Mount Mansfield. Resorts in Vermont that once entertained only summer visitors now offered winter activities as well.

During World War II, many of Vermont's women entered the workforce for the first time.

During World War II (1939–1945), 50,000 of Vermont's men and women served in the U.S. armed forces. Those at home also helped in the war effort. Granite workers used their skills to build chains for warship anchors. Women farmed or made machinery in factories. Children gathered milkweed pods to stuff life jackets and collected scrap paper, tin, copper, and brass for making war supplies.

In the years since World War II, Vermont has earned most of its money from manufacturing and tourism. But because Vermont does not have large cities, the state has a hard time attracting big companies. As a result, workers in Vermont tend to earn lower wages than workers in other parts of the country. So Vermonters are looking for ways to improve their state's economy.

**Vermont's slopes are a
leading tourist attraction.**

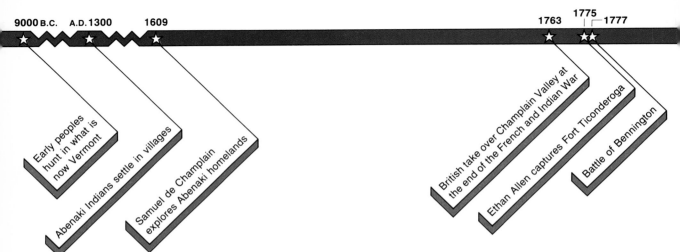

9000 B.C.   A.D. 1300   1609   1763   1775   1777

Early peoples hunt in what is now Vermont

Abenaki Indians settle in villages

Samuel de Champlain explores Abenaki homelands

British take over Champlain Valley at the end of the French and Indian War

Ethan Allen captures Fort Ticonderoga

Battle of Bennington

Some Vermonters hope to bring larger manufacturing companies into the state. Others would like to increase the number of small companies and encourage more tourism. But most residents agree that in Vermont's 200 years of statehood, the state has known hard times before and will overcome these challenges as well.

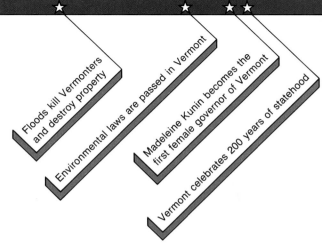

| 1791 | 1812 | 1865 | 1927 | 1970 | 1985 | 1991 |

Vermont becomes the 14th state

War of 1812 begins (1812–1815)

Vermont's machine-tool industry is booming

Floods kill Vermonters and destroy property

Environmental laws are passed in Vermont

Madeleine Kunin becomes the first female governor of Vermont

Vermont celebrates 200 years of statehood

From 1985 to 1991, Madeleine Kunin was the first woman to serve as Vermont's governor.

41

Living and Working in Vermont

Most of Vermont's early settlers lived in the countryside, far from their neighbors. Families had to rely on their own hard work to survive. Sometimes, though, friends got together for special tasks, such as husking corn, building barns, or making quilts.

Nowadays, Vermonters are less isolated than the early settlers, but they are just as independent. More than two-thirds of Vermont's residents still live in the countryside or in small towns tucked away in valleys or on hillsides.

With about 500,000 inhabitants, Vermont has fewer people than most other states in the nation. Even Vermont's largest city, Burlington, has less than 40,000 people. The second largest city, Rutland, has half as many people as Burlington. Other cities include Barre, Bennington, Brattleboro, and Montpelier—the state capital.

Most Vermonters were born in the United States and have European backgrounds. About half are descendants of settlers from Britain and France.

A family carves pumpkins in Cavendish, Vermont.

43

Some farmers in Vermont grow apples.

Many Vermonters have German, Scottish, Polish, Swedish, or Dutch roots. African Americans, Native Americans, Asian Americans, and **Latinos** have the smallest populations in the state. Together they make up less than 1 percent of Vermont's residents.

About 2,500 Abenaki live in Vermont. To preserve the ways of their ancestors, Indians in the state hold special events, such as a fall harvest celebration. Some Abenaki

A quilter in Vermont displays her work.

teach their children the Abenaki language. Others visit schools to present information about Abenaki culture to young Vermonters.

Like the Abenaki, many other Vermonters practice skills passed on by their families. In fact, Vermont is known for its artists and craftspeople, who hold workshops to teach others their skills. Quilters, weavers, painters, sculptors, and potters sell their work at craft centers throughout the state.

Old-fashioned buildings add charm to Main Street in Hardwick, Vermont.

In many villages and towns, well-kept old buildings give Vermont the look and feel of an earlier time.

Artist Norman Rockwell captured this old-time look on covers he painted for a magazine called the

Saturday Evening Post. Rockwell lived in Arlington, Vermont, for several years and used the town and its people as his models.

Vermont has many different museums devoted to showing the state's history. Exhibits feature everything from old machine tools to farm life in the 1700s to modern dairying. Some museums offer a firsthand look at workers on the job—cutting granite, carving marble, or making cheese, ice cream, or apple cider. At sugaring time, visitors at Vermont's sugarhouses can watch as guides collect sap from maple trees and boil it to make maple syrup.

The Bennington Museum, in Bennington, displays the works of one of the town's most famous residents—Anna Mary Robertson Moses, better known as Grandma Moses. This self-taught artist started painting at the age of 76. She continued to paint scenes of New England country life until her death at the age of 101.

Vermont's farmers boil sap in sugarhouses to make syrup. About 35 gallons (132 liters) of sap make 1 gallon (3.8 l) of maple syrup.

In Shelburne, Vermont, a reconstruction of an early American settlement shows visitors how the colonists lived. The Shelburne Museum features 36 buildings from the 1700s, including houses, a country store, a lighthouse, and a huge paddle-wheel boat that once steamed around Lake Champlain. Printers, weavers, basketmakers, and other craftspeople at the museum demonstrate their talents and hold workshops for visitors.

Vermont's hills ring with the sounds of music during outdoor summer concerts. Fairs and special events celebrate traditional music with fiddlers and banjo-pickers who play folk tunes that the early settlers once played.

Vermonters and tourists alike can visit the original steamship *Ticonderoga* *(left)*, built in 1906, and listen to folk musicians *(above)* at music festivals.

49

Campers canoe across a lake in eastern Vermont.

Vermont's great outdoors attracts many people. Both residents and out-of-state visitors enjoy biking Vermont's peaceful back roads and climbing its mountains. Hikers follow a variety of trails, including abandoned rail beds and old logging roads. The most famous footpath is the Long Trail, which winds along the peaks of the Green Mountains from Massachusetts, through Vermont, and up to Canada.

The state's fast-running rivers provide white-water rafters with an adventure. Vermont's lakes and rivers offer sailing and fishing. On Lake Champlain, scuba divers can explore old sunken ships!

Ever since the first vacationers came to Vermont in the mid-1800s, visitors have flocked to the state to ski and to admire the scenery. Thousands of service workers help these visitors enjoy their stay. Service workers greet vacationers at national and state forests, check in people at motels and ski resorts, serve meals at restaurants, and pump gas at service stations.

Horseback riders enjoy Vermont's trails.

Other Vermonters with service jobs include salesclerks, bank tellers, teachers, and doctors. Vermont's government workers also are part of the state's service industry. Altogether, three out of four Vermonters have service jobs.

About one out of every six Vermonters work in manufacturing, and factories account for most of the state's earnings. At plants around Burlington, workers produce computers and computer software. Manufactured items in other parts of the state include granite monuments, teddy bears, flashlights, dishes, glassware, tools, clothing, guns, and furniture.

Although farms cover more than one-fifth of the state's land, only about 1 out of 25 people work in

agriculture. Dairy farms supply milk and cream to Vermont's cheesemakers as well as to Boston and southeastern New England. Cheddar cheese, apples, and apple cider are important farm products, and most of the country's maple syrup comes from Vermont.

Vermont's dairy cows
(facing page) **provide milk,
while the state's quarries**
(right) **supply granite
and marble.**

Protecting the Environment

Vermonters are proud of the rustic beauty of their state—its winding roads, covered bridges, tiny villages, and hillside farms. Vermont's picture-postcard charm is the reason many residents choose to live there.

Natural beauty also makes the state attractive to visitors. Every year thousands of out-of-state vacationers travel to Vermont. These visitors need places to eat and sleep and safe roads on which to drive.

Some tourists enjoy the state so much they buy vacation homes in Vermont. Year-round residents also expect well-kept roads and want comfortable homes.

More than 100 covered bridges add to the beauty of Vermont's countryside.

Some people buy summer cottages in Vermont.

To meet the needs of residents and vacationers, land developers buy land on which to build homes and to cut ski trails. But some Vermonters question how much land should be used in this way. Too much development can harm the environment.

Some Vermonters fear, for example, that cutting down trees to make ski trails on mountains will cause soil **erosion**. This wearing away of the earth's surface happens mostly in spring and summer, when melting snow and rain carry away soil. When the trees still stood, their roots helped hold the soil in place.

When workers cut ski trails on Vermont's mountains, many animals lose their homes.

Protecting Black Bears

When you think of a bear, you might imagine a strong, wild animal that is dangerous to humans. But people can actually be more of a threat to bears. In Vermont, black bears are found in forests and mountains, where they live undisturbed by people. Experts fear that the state's black bears might lose their habitats (homes) to land developers.

Black bears need a lot of space in which to live and search for food. Roaming miles and miles each day, they nibble on nuts, berries, and insects. Black bears also need plenty of drinking water and safe dens for sleeping. But when developers build houses, condominiums, or roads in bear habitats, the bears have trouble finding food and shelter.

To discover exactly where black bears live and wander, experts look for the signs that bears leave behind. Sometimes researchers find teeth marks on tree trunks. Other times, they discover claw marks on a "baby-sitter tree," where a mother bear leaves her cubs for safety while she hunts. These clues about bear habitats help officials identify areas to protect from development.

Studying bear habitats is the first step in protecting Vermont's black bears. Experts are also working hard to educate land developers and residents about bear habitats. With these efforts, Vermonters hope to ensure a safe future for the state's black bears.

Some Vermonters also worry that building many houses close together will cause too much wear and tear on existing roads. And building more roads can disturb wildlife habitats and loosen the soil, causing more erosion.

Because of these concerns, Vermont has passed strict environmental laws. The laws allow some development to take place, but they also protect Vermont's natural beauty.

One law makes it difficult to subdivide large pieces of land. This means owners must get permission to break the land into smaller lots to sell to individual buyers. The subdividing might lead to overdevelopment if these buyers were to build homes on the small lots.

Vermont's environmental laws protect towns from overdevelopment, too. Developers must build in places that have a plentiful supply of water and a safe way to get rid of waste. And the new development cannot bring more people or traffic to an area than the community can handle.

A Vermont law forbids big billboards that hide the state's scenery. Small wooden signs point the way instead.

The laws also protect scenic roads, waterways, and other features of Vermont's landscape. But not everyone agrees on which areas should be protected. What is important to one person—a stretch of woods or a winding creek—might not be to another.

For example, the laws that control development have caused problems for some of Vermont's farmers. Many owners of small farms have a hard time making a good living. The cost of running a farm is high, and some farmers cannot make enough money to pay all of their bills. These farmers want to make a profit by selling their land to developers.

Before Vermont's environmental laws were passed, selling farmland to developers was fairly easy. But now, with so many limits in place, developers are much less likely to buy land from a farmer than before the laws were passed.

With the new laws, farmers are wondering what to do. Those hoping to sell their land to developers are upset by the laws. But homeowners who do not want the areas around them developed further welcome the limits. As the discussion continues over how much development is good for Vermont, many Vermonters are working to preserve the state's rustic beauty for future generations to enjoy.

Vermonters are striving to protect the beauty of their state.

Vermont's Famous People

George Perkins Marsh (1801–1882) wrote an influential book in 1864 called *Man and Nature,* which introduced the idea of conserving land and wildlife for future generations. He was born in Woodstock, Vermont.

Clarina Nichols (1810–1885), a newspaper editor from West Townshend, Vermont, was an outspoken women's rights leader. In many articles, she argued that women should be able to inherit and own property as men could. Her efforts led government officials to pass laws granting women many new property rights in the 1800s.

Homer St. Francis (born 1935), chief of the Abenaki nation, has worked for 30 years to reclaim Vermont for the Abenaki Indians, whose land was taken without a treaty. St. Francis also has preserved the Abenaki's hunting and fishing rights.

◀ CLARINA NICHOLS

HOMER ST. FRANCIS ▶

◀ LARKIN MEAD

THOMAS WATERMAN WOOD ▼

ARTISTS

Larkin Mead (1835–1910) was an artist who grew up in Brattleboro, Vermont. Mead sculpted a statue of Ethan Allen for Vermont's State House in 1861. He also created a statue of Allen for the U.S. Capitol building in Washington, D.C.

Thomas Waterman Wood (1823–1903), a painter, created portraits of famous New Yorkers and painted scenes of African Americans during the Civil War. Born in Montpelier, he founded the T. W. Wood Art Gallery in his hometown.

EDUCATORS

John Dewey (1859–1952) was an educator and philosopher from Burlington. He believed that students learn best by experimenting, instead of by memorizing facts. Dewey's ideas helped shape the nation's educational system.

Emma Hart Willard (1787–1870) established a girls' school at her home in Middlebury, Vermont, in 1814. She proved that girls could learn science, philosophy, and other subjects that, in her day, were taught only to men. Willard later founded the Troy Female Seminary, which prepared women to be teachers.

▲ JOHN DEWEY

▲ EMMA HART WILLARD

JOHN DEERE ▶

INVENTORS

John Deere (1804–1886) was a blacksmith who invented the first steel plow. His device made plowing easier and faster by turning heavy soil without getting clogged with dirt. By 1868 his firm, Deere and Company, was producing many types of farm machinery. Deere was born in Rutland, Vermont.

Elisha Graves Otis (1811–1861), from Halifax, Vermont, helped make elevators safe and popular. A master mechanic, Otis invented a safety device that could stop an elevator if its lifting rope broke.

MUSICIANS

Maria von Trapp (1905–1987) was a musician from Austria who moved with her family to Stowe, Vermont, in 1942. Her marriage to Baron Georg von Trapp and their family's escape from the Nazis was made famous in the movie *The Sound of Music*.

◀ MARIA VON TRAPP

Rudy Vallee (1901–1986), a singer and saxophonist, was born in Island Pond, Vermont. He is best known for crooning his theme song, "My Time Is Your Time," into a megaphone. In 1961 Vallee appeared in a play called *How to Succeed in Business Without Really Trying.*

◀ RUDY VALLEE

CALVIN
▼ COOLIDGE

POLITICAL LEADERS

Chester A. Arthur (1829–1886) was the nation's 21st president. Vice president under James Garfield, Arthur became president in 1881 after Garfield was assassinated. He was born in Fairfield, Vermont.

◀ ALEXANDER
TWILIGHT

JOSEPH
SMITH ▶

Calvin Coolidge (1872–1933), born in Plymouth Notch, Vermont, became the 30th president of the United States after the death of President Warren G. Harding in 1923. Known as Silent Cal for his quiet manner, Coolidge led the nation during the 1920s.

Alexander Twilight (1795–1857) was born in Corinth, Vermont. After receiving a degree from Vermont's Middlebury College in 1823, Twilight became the country's first black college graduate. Elected to the Vermont legislature in 1836, he was the nation's first African American state legislator.

RELIGIOUS LEADERS

Joseph Smith (1805–1844), born in Sharon, Vermont, was the founder of the Mormon church—also called the Church of Jesus Christ of Latter-day Saints. In 1830 he published *The Book of Mormon,* which is the Mormons' holy book.

64

Brigham Young (1801–1877) became the leader of the Mormons in 1844. He led his followers to Utah, where they could practice their faith freely. Born in Whitingham, Vermont, Young founded Utah's first towns, factories, and schools.

SPORTS FIGURES

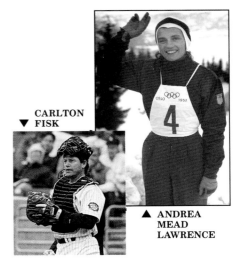

CARLTON
▼ FISK

▲ ANDREA
MEAD
LAWRENCE

Carlton Fisk (born 1947) was one of the greatest catchers in baseball history. After 11 seasons with the Boston Red Sox, Fisk moved to the Chicago White Sox in 1981. His major-league records include most games caught and most home runs hit by a catcher. Fisk was born in Bellows Falls, Vermont.

Andrea Mead Lawrence (born 1932) began skiing in her backyard in Rutland, Vermont, at the age of four. In the 1952 Olympic Games, she became the first woman to win two gold medals in skiing. Lawrence earned her Olympic medals in the slalom and giant slalom events.

◀ E. ANNIE PROULX

KATHERINE ▶
PATERSON

WRITERS

Katherine Paterson (born 1932) is a children's book author from Barre, Vermont, who has won two National Book Awards and two Newbery Medals. Among her best-known novels are *Bridge to Terabithia* and *Jacob Have I Loved*. Paterson's books have been published in 18 languages.

E. Annie Proulx (born 1935) has published several novels, as well as many stories and articles for national magazines. In 1994 she won a Pulitzer Prize for her novel *The Shipping News*. Proulx lives in Vershire, Vermont.

Facts-at-a-Glance

Nickname: Green Mountain State
Song: "Hail, Vermont!"
Motto: Freedom and Unity
Flower: red clover
Tree: sugar maple
Bird: hermit thrush

Population: 562,758*
Rank in population, nationwide: 49th
Area: 9,615 sq mi (24,903 sq km)
Rank in area, nationwide: 45th
Date and ranking of statehood:
   March 4, 1791, the 14th state
Capital: Montpelier
Major cities (and populations*):
   Burlington (39,127), Rutland (18,230),
   South Burlington (12,809), Barre (9,482),
   Essex Junction (8,396), Montpelier (8,247)
U.S. senators: 2
U.S. representatives: 1
Electoral votes: 3

Places to visit: Bennington Battle Monument in Bennington, Vermont Marble Exhibit in Proctor, Rock of Ages granite quarry in Barre, Maple Grove Maple Museum and Factory in Saint Johnsbury, Calvin Coolidge Birthplace in Plymouth Notch

Annual events: Stowe Winter Carnival in Stowe (Jan.), Vermont Maple Festival in Saint Albans (April), Balloon Festival and Crafts Fair in Quechee (June), Vermont Quilt Festival in Northfield (July), Championship Old-Time Fiddlers Contest in Bellows Falls (Aug.), Fall Foliage Festival in Barre (Oct.)

*1990 census

66

Natural resources: granite, marble, slate, limestone, gravel, talc, forests

Agricultural products: milk, butter, cheese, maple syrup, maple sugar, apples, potatoes, eggs, Christmas trees, beef cattle, sheep, poultry, hay

Manufactured goods: computers, flashlights, machine tools, printed materials, food products, lumber and wood products, teddy bears

ENDANGERED SPECIES
Mammals—lynx, eastern mountain lion
Birds—common loon, osprey, bald eagle, peregrine falcon, loggerhead shrike, Henslow's sparrow, spruce grouse, common tern
Reptiles—timber rattlesnake
Fish—lake sturgeon, northern brook lamprey
Plants—Boott's rattlesnake root, swamp birch, climbing fern, Champlain beach grass, needle-spine rose

WHERE VERMONTERS WORK
Services—56 percent
   (services includes jobs in trade; community, social & personal services; finance, insurance, & real estate; transportation, communication, & utilities)
Manufacturing—18 percent
Government—15 percent
Construction—7 percent
Agriculture—4 percent

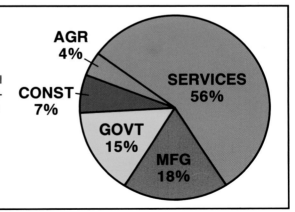

AGR
4%
CONST
7%
SERVICES
56%
GOVT
15%
MFG
18%

PRONUNCIATION GUIDE

Abenaki (a-buh-NAH-kee)

Barre (BEHR-ee)

Brattleboro (BRAT-uhl-buhr-uh)

Champlain (sham-PLAYN)

Connecticut (kuh-NEHD-uh-kuht)

Iroquois (IHR-uh-kwoy)

Montpelier (mahnt-PEEL-yuhr)

Petoubouque (BIHT-uh-bahk)

Taconic (tuh-KAWN-ihk)

Ticonderoga (ty-kahn-duhr-OH-guh)

Winooski (wuh-NOO-skee)

Glossary

colony A territory ruled by a country some distance away.

constitution The system of basic laws or rules of a government, society, or organization. The document in which these laws or rules are written.

erosion The wearing away of the earth's surface by the forces of water, wind, or ice.

glacier A large body of ice and snow that moves slowly over land.

immigrant A person who moves into a foreign country and settles there.

Latino A person living in the United States who either came from or has ancestors from Latin America. Latin America includes Mexico and most of Central and South America.

missionary A person sent out by a religious group to spread its beliefs to other people.

precipitation Rain, snow, and other forms of moisture that fall to earth.

quarry An open pit dug by miners for obtaining limestone, marble, slate, granite, or other building stone.

Index

Acknowledgments:

Maryland Cartographics, Inc., pp. 2, 11; NE Stock Photo: Effin Older, pp. 2–3, 44, 49 (inset), Margo Taussig Pinkerton, p. 45, Art Phaneuf, p. 50; Jane P. Downton / Root Resources, p. 6; Jack Lindstrom, p. 7; Erwin C. "Bud" Nielsen, Tucson, AZ, p. 8; Jerry Hennen, pp. 9, 12, 15; Carolyn Bates, pp. 10, 16, 53; Vermont Department of Travel & Tourism, pp. 13, 14, 17, 48–49, 68, 71; Mae Scanlan, p. 18; Special Collections, University of Vermont Library, pp. 19, 20, 21, 25; Library of Congress, pp. 23, 26, 62 (top), 64 (center right and bottom right); *The American Revolution,* Dover Publications, p. 27; Betty Groskin, pp. 29, 51, 52; Vermont Historical Society, pp. 31, 33, 36–37; Brattleboro Photos, Inc., p. 34; Russell Vermontiana Collection, p. 38; © Thomas P. Benincas, Jr., pp. 39, 47, 57; U.S. Department of Education, p. 41; © Gerry Lemmo, pp. 43, 46, 56, 59; Kay Shaw Photography, pp. 54–55; Habitat Researcher, Susan Morse, p. 58 (both); Charles F. Swenson, p. 61; The Sovereign Abenaki Nation, p. 62 (center); *Dictionary of American Portraits,* pp. 62 (bottom left), 63 (top left and top right); T. W. Wood Art Gallery, Montpelier, VT, p. 62 (bottom right); Deere & Company, p. 63 (center); Frank L. Forward / Trapp Family Lodge, p. 63 (bottom); Hollywood Book & Poster, p. 64 (top); Orleans County (VT) Historical Society, p. 64 (center); UPI / Bettmann, p. 65 (top right); Chicago White Sox, p. 65 (top left); Vyto Starinskas, Rutland Daily Herald / Macmillan Publishing, p. 65 (bottom left); Jill Paton Walsh, p. 65 (bottom right); Jean Matheny, p. 66.